FROM THE DARK

FROM THE DARK

poems by Len Roberts

State University of New York Press   ALBANY

ACKNOWLEDGMENTS

My thanks to the editors and publishers of the following magazines in which some of these poems appeared: *Alabama University Review of the Arts, California Quarterly, Carolina Quarterly, Dark Horse, Ironwood, Kansas Quarterly, Long Pond Review, the minnesota review, The Missouri Review, Momentum, Northwest Review, The Ohio Review, Poetry Australia, Poetry Miscellany, Poetry Now, Prairie Schooner, Quarterly West, The Southern Poetry Review, The Texas Review,* and *West Branch.*

I wish to thank especially Ken Delahunty, Gerald Stern, and C. K. Williams for their valuable suggestions about the original drafts of many of these poems, and for their continual encouragement and friendship.

I also want to thank the Pennsylvania Council on the Arts for its Poetry Fellowship, and Northhampton County Area Community College for its sabbatical—both of which gave me some of the time and money I needed to complete this book.

Published by
State University of New York Press, Albany
© 1984 State University of New York
All rights reserved
Printed in the United States of America
No part of this book may be used or reproduced
in any manner whatsoever without written permission
except in the case of brief quotations embodied in
critical articles and reviews.
For information, address State University of New York
Press, State University Plaza, Albany, N.Y., 12246
Library of Congress Cataloging in Publication Data
Roberts, Len, 1947–
    From the dark.
    (SUNY poetry series)
    I. Title. II. Series.
PS3568.02389F7   1984   811'.54   83-4908
ISBN 0-87395-757-1
ISBN 0-87395-758-X (pbk.)

10 9 8 7 6 5 4 3 2 1

CONTENTS

I. THE FORGIVING

Six Suns   3
First Kiss   4
The Forgiving   5
The Snow Family   7
Pyracantha   8
Homer   9
Peanut Butter and Jelly Sandwiches   10
Washing the Windows   11
Blacktop Work   12
Hearing the Girl Story While Shoveling Snow   13
Brothers   14
My Father's Whistle   16
Cohoes Falls   17
The Garden   18
Stealing   19
The Cellar   20

II. THE ENCOURAGING SEA

An Apology   23
Waiting for Her to Wake   24
Lines of Rain   25
The Encouraging Sea   26
Considering the House   27
Waking and Remembering a Family Cemetery in Maine   28
On Big John's Hill   29
White Pigeon   30
The Diver and the Coal   31

Children Singing   32
Wind Over Land   33
Another Journey   34

III. FIRST ROOMS

Riding Out To See the First Flowers   37
Pip   38
Watching the Moon   39
Dear Mother   40
It Will Wait   41
The Unborn   42
Joshua   43
The Difference   44
The Indian Maiden   45
First Rooms   46

IV. PARTISAN

Partisan   49
Stone Builder on Hvar   50
Vide Unfolding Nets   51
Old Woman on Hvar   52
One Dream of Two Red Starfish   53
Enjoying the English Countryside   54
Hercules' Temple at Paestum   55
The Rape of the Sabine Women   56
Walking Through a Family Graveyard and Thinking of the Italian
    Stone Builders   57
Behind the Counter at a Soda Shop in Florence   58
Catching Eels   59

For Bradford, David, and Joshua

I. THE FORGIVING

THE FORGIVING

for James Wright

1. Listening to the August cicadas,
   I remember *the mysterious lives of the poor,*
   Mrs. Polisviet's knees turning to butter
   as she washes down First National's marble steps,
   Ziggy, bumping his head, wandering three days
   before he finds the river, or Donna
   swallowing sperm for a dollar a head,
   crawling the back row of the Cohoes Theater.

   Less than fifteen miles down this lake shore
   I sat below the Fort watching July 4th fireworks,
   leaned over, cupped Mary's breast, promised
   our children would not grow up naked.
   All that night she was cold,
   her thick hair sprawled on the pillow;
   the next morning she was gone.
   Still some nights her green robe opens
   and I lie down to lick her clean,
   but hear my cousin, Julie,
   her seven-year-old throat singing
   from the dirt hole behind the American Bowling Alley
   as eleven boys, shirts still on,
   hide themselves in her body.

   The moon's face floats on the mountain.
   I wonder how many eyes have burned back the light,
   how many lovers have walked into bushes or fields,
   dry leaves crackling under body weight;
   if many looked back, walking sideways like crabs in deep water,
   if many bowed, wishing they had more to offer.

2. I place the spoon of instant coffee into the yellow cup
   as pre-dawn mist drifts a foot above the lake
   and black ants carry their dead over the green rocks, twigs, rust
       needles,
   into the dark holes and crevices.
   Near the greasy rocks that form a ledge from island to island,
   the pine stump floats, polished, near-weightless,
   the brackish moss soft, feathers whitening,

spread under pines, no body, no beak or claws;
the sun quivers a yellow line on waves toward me,
a gull glides into the green mountain.

Where are they now, the ghosts,
worm-gatherers, silent ones under gray stones,
the one-eyed boy with squirrel's hat perched on his head,
the deep featherbed brought from Germany that we'd sink in
while violin music played down the alley?
Come out, you, girl I first kissed
that night we hid in the blue dark of Big John's orchard,
and you, Porky, flattening your penis against the window
that morning I knocked to play poker.
No one's awake, the crow crackles,
a yellow finch, two thumbs big, hops from leaf to leaf.
Twenty years begin closing like a circular wound,
from the inside out, skin stretching membrane
like this morning's clear water surface, rippling.

The sun lights windows on the far shore,
the red gazebo fills with shadows.
I bend to the inch-thick moss,
finger yellow buds, red tips,
acknowledging my debts.

THE SNOW FAMILY

Heavy white woods and
green cakes of ice. Suddenly
my father rises from his last bed
to look my brothers and me in the face again.
Nick starts shoveling a clear, round spot
because he can't find his mind;
Ray goes out for hot dogs
and we know he won't be back.
—Sitting on the cold rock I remember our mother
saying I'll get piles,
but she's not here now, and I wonder why not.
She was there in the warm kitchen
boiling spaghetti, frying fish cakes,
screaming that he was drunk, drunk,
and didn't make enough. She
was there in the blue bathrobe
she wore to every bar in Cohoes,
tender still, looking for him.
If she comes this time, she'll wear
the Navy-blue and white polka-dot dress
and she'll be slim. This time
we'll all stop our chores
and go up to her in the ten-degree air,
say "You look beautiful. Where
have you been?"

PYRACANTHA

As we lay in the eighth-grade clothes closet
with the snow-soaked coats and wet rubber boots,
I told the immigrant girl, Renate,
she was beautiful. For proof,
I gave her my rabbit's foot,
all I had to keep me from the fears I'd grown into—
that the dark was alive those quiet Sunday afternoons
I'd fall asleep listening to my mother
in the kitchen; the sense
of disappearing, even then,
into the graying light
that would become my life.

Walking home last night in the November cold—
the chrysanthemums beginning to wilt brown,
only the pyracantha, the fire-thorn,
alive in the snow—
I felt the seed of some old cry
begin in my throat, without words
because there were none.
Not for Renate's small, hard breasts,
nor for her hair combed back so tight
it looked as though it hurt,
and not for the years between;
not even for her mother,
who sat with us, night after night
in that dim parlor reading,
telling us in the few English words she knew
that we should take our studies seriously
and be wise.

HOMER

Yellow sparks flew into the gray
Pennsylvania sky as he bent into the mouths
of Buicks, great-winged DeSotos, milk trucks,
flatbeds, Chryslers, his hood pulled up,
goggles going black from breath and smoke.
Hot days he'd come to the house every hour,
blue work shirt hanging wet to back and chest,
pants forming shadows on both sides
of his crotch, and he'd sit a few minutes
drinking well water, staring out the window
down to where the twisted, piled-up shapes waited.
Some mornings I'd go with him,
try to walk the way he did, that mix
of man and cow's gait, and I'd talk,
ask what flower that was by the heap of tires,
what kind of tree near the wire,
what vine choking it. I wanted to ask
why he thought his daughter was a whore
because she dated boys, or how he'd spent the night
he'd told his son to leave because his hair had grown
too long, and the son did leave,
only to wrap his car around a telephone pole
an hour later. But he'd be quiet, like the fields
he plowed, so I listened to our feet pad the dust,
looked out at the mass of junk and felt
the stillness of those late summer nights
when he'd come by with baby rabbits
in his long farmer's pockets, line us up
one by one, let us hold the warm,
shaking bodies we were so afraid of.

PEANUT BUTTER AND JELLY SANDWICHES

While my father cuts his way
through canebrake on Guadalcanal
and my mother balances the $40-a-week budget,
I step into the blank space
at the kitchen table and begin making
sandwiches for my two brothers and myself,
smearing peanut butter until it tears
the bread, scraping gobs of quivering jelly,
licking the knife when no one is looking. I
am thinking only of how to fold the wax paper neatly
over the finished sandwiches, how to crease
the paper once, tuck the ends in to seal it shut.
—There are so many miles unwinding inside me
and hours of lying on a pebbled ocean beach;
and there is David, and Mary,
an old man rocking on creaking linoleum,
a day's walk up a holy mountain. No wonder
I hold each sandwich to the light
to see jelly leaking, brown specks of peanut butter
stuck to wax, that I place each one down
into the open-mouthed brown bags like a body
set gently into its grave, stacking them
like balanced blocks, one by one, for tomorrow.

WASHING THE WINDOWS

One Sunday every Spring he'd open
the window, climb out on the ledge
twenty feet over the sidewalk and cobblestones,
Tommy Edwards' songs blasting,
and he'd whistle, hanging on with one thin hand,
as he washed the windows with the other.
I never once heard my mother
tell him not to do it,
and I was always the first one out,
hiding behind the 1952 Buick,
to watch the moccasins, white socks
and khaki pants drift from the window.
The neighbors walked by and said hello
as though he were sitting on the porch smoking
the way he did other Sunday mornings,
and the drivers honked, everybody smiling
because he perched on that sill.
We had a ladder. He didn't have to
whistle over stone, only a few feet
of brick and the edge of a tar roof
between him and the morning blue sky.
He didn't have to float there, free
but holding back, one hand wrapped
around the wooden frame,
the other hand rubbing each pane invisible.

BLACKTOP WORK

for my grandfather

Some Monday mornings I still
hear the beat of the tamp, the click
of rake as you work the blacktop into the shape
of driveway, sidewalk, or patch in the road,
the spit and sputter of old Leo as he hawkers
into the red bandanna unloosened
from his coiled neck, the groan
of the hydraulic jack as it lifts and drops
those tons of blacktop onto the ground.
So much blackness shifting like waves
hitting off some beach you'd never seen
but often heard the music of, and then you
lifting the rake into whatever sky
and bringing it down with the glittering sound
of your breath giving and keeping time.
That was work! the bills at home forgotten,
and the corns burning inside shoes empty
with holes, the nights you needed more
than one shot at Boney's Bar before
you could walk through the dark
toward the brown porch. So
easily you appear again at the end of summer,
rake in your left hand stretched before you,
right hand forming the smallest cradle
that pulls and pushes from your gut
to form the music that says you were here.

12

HEARING THE GIRL STORY
WHILE SHOVELING SNOW

The cobblestones gleam as the snow flakes fall,
softly piling until they are two or three feet high
and we go out with our shovels. It is then the boy at my side,
steaming, cheeks red, tells me he plays strip poker
with young Irene until she's bare. I
am eleven and cannot stop shoveling, for this is the way my father
    works, and his father,
and the neighbors watch and shout, "He will be a bull like the other
    Roberts."
And when we sit down on the brown porch, men and boys sweating
    although it is below zero,
they don't pass the wine bottle by me, but let me hold it to the
    winter-starred sky and drink.
I watch them, the French-Canadians, the Poles, and German DP's,
hear them say the snow will fall a few more hours,
that they will have to meet again early tomorrow morning to break
    their backs shoveling
so they can get out of the block.
The way they say it means it is the most dreaded work, yet
they are smiling, and I am smiling too, thinking of my friend
    watching Irene's body,
until one of the men starts humming, and my father takes his
    gloves off to play the harmonica
while they talk about the bitterness of other winters in the old
    country,
when the snow rose so much higher, and it was so much colder,
and they were young and didn't care.

BROTHERS

What mad mother, softly rocking, rising
and falling, stretched her mouth open again,
and yet again, so that we might pass down
from father to father to father?

Pass down what?

The man dragging Raymond down
to the Mohawk River, putting a knife to his throat,
making him suck.
The terror of the long walk home, the crying
on the table top, under the bulb,
our mother saying now he'll be a queer.
One had to turn away, to stare
at cracked squares of linoleum, tin flowers
indented on walls; any image,
clearly; her hands, worn,
veined, holding his balls,
her head bent so close,
her hate, her words,
unretractable.

And Nicholas, floating over Okinawa, testing
Goldfarb parachutes for the Marines, one
afternoon looked at the sun—
that was all he could remember, he said, but
when he hit the ground he forgot how to land
and his calf bones went through the knees.
Nicholas, who gets drunk every Friday night,
believing again he is an angel,
whose name means "the Great" in Russian, who sleeps
in one room, throws his clothes into an old rainbarrel
he dragged from the alley as a valuable antique,
who sees St. Bernard's grotto where he climbed once to look the
    Virgin in the eye
and tell her he really meant it;
who walks past Golden Eagle where his father worked eighteen
    years, embezzled money and died alone,
who goes over the bridge where his young friend leaped because his

wife left and took the child,
who looks down at the water in the cold air of a Cohoes winter,
pushes hands deeper into pockets to keep warm, dares
to think, Lord, how we suffer.

MY FATHER'S WHISTLE

One night as I lay on the green hill
watching the first gray of night cover
the city, I heard your whistle calling me home,
that slow music swimming from your throat.
I didn't go. Instead,
I watched the ants divide the bread,
I listened to their thin legs scratch the earth.
I let them live
and didn't go home for more than twenty years.
When I did, I saw the chrysanthemums
stained on the wall, the tin ceiling cracking,
the pear tree I'd climbed split by lightning;
I could hear you murmuring in bed,
her voice twisting as she shouted,
the soft click of the door
behind you.
And the backyards darkening,
dirt clouds as we walked,
the sound of the owl, that grave digger,
breaking in
just as you disappeared through the white
pickets, the climbing yellow rose, your heart.

COHOES FALLS

Cold trees, ash, oak, birch, shagbark hickory, white roots
go down into the cold earth, tap-rooted,
touching the center.
I am drunk again, wondering at dead leaves still
in the still air, under the moon and sun,
and gray reflections on the scummy water and the dreams
 of summer.
Soon each thing will come out of its life into more life,
and more, and more again, until,
again, there is nothing but the breath stirring
ash leaves, the few distinct ripples on the river,
the hairs on my arm.

There, on the rock hanging over Cohoes Falls,
blue-black slate, water
breaking, foaming, then falling,
no sounds except our arms, heavy,
splashing through the river
and then our climbing out into the night,
and you lying back, knees up,
me entering as you cried and cried.

Lover, sister, mother, woman, air, earth, fire, water

you are not now what you were and I am not what I was and the
 trees
are gone, cut, bulldozed, burned.
Only the bare river remains, soft mud in shallows, cattails
 persisting as though against a great weight.

THE GARDEN

You would put on a dark blue and white polka-dot
dress, imitation pearl earrings and necklace,
sit before the mirror combing your hair
until it was perfect, never understanding
why people hurt you. Then
you went out to buy flowers at Rosa's,
moving among men smoking pipes, women
with babies, your body tense in sunlight.
Mother, you needed a garden
where you could have hidden, where
your hands might have felt
the cool dirt you seeded
with cucumbers and beans, radishes and zinnias, anything
but those irregular white stones
you painted summer after summer.
Yes, a garden with a radio, a glass
of iced water, or lemoned tea,
a chair, a book;
where the light might have touched your shoulder
and you could have jumped, afraid, until you had become
accustomed to being so softly touched,
and then could have undressed, lay back
in your startling white skin.

STEALING

Last night I woke in the dark knowing
my father was with me,
like the night I stole down the cold hall stairs
to take change from his breadman's purse,
the green work pants hung on the peg,
boots placed neatly under the chair,
and then, as I hushed the click inside my shirt,
his soft breathing as I looked up
to see the lit cigarette rising and falling.
I don't wonder anymore
that he didn't sleep nights
only to rise before light
to perk coffee, shave, whistling
with the low tunes of the radio.
I don't need to call him back from peddling bread
in the three-foot drifts
to ask how he could forgive
that night gathering now in my chest,
or how he could make me take
the coins he placed gently into my hands,
and silently wave me away.

THE CELLAR

In the damp and coal-dusted
cellar, with the flat cans of black shoe polish,
rags, molding newspapers and discarded
tools, I read my first books, *Robinson Cruesoe,*
The Tale of Two Cities, Avalanche, Ivanhoe.
Scratching from poison ivy, the burst bubbles
of poison streaming my skin,
I climbed down every morning with books piling
my arms, my face wrecking whole cities
of webs.
—At ten I had left my mother and father
and brothers behind me. I had jumped ship
without even knowing it and settled
in this very land.

II. THE ENCOURAGING SEA

AN APOLOGY

Soon you will have to scream to me from the garden
where the dried corn stalks rattle in the winter wind
before I abandon the wooden ladder and Skil saw,
the solid oak beams holding up the floors.
You will have to bang on the newly painted green shutters,
float your voice in over the hammer,
tell me as though for the first time
about the triangle earrings and the black enamel heart,
the old man who walks between the dried rows of vegetables
    until it is too dark.
It must be you, when I'm so tired I can't get up to put another log
    into the stove,
who will whisper about the red rose dish, or the original Ming
    roosters,
or the thick mascara spread on my blue sweater.
And if I get up at 5 a.m. to eat cold hamburger and drink warm soda
and then come back to stare at the cast-iron Indian Maiden just now
    coming out of the dark,
it will have to be you who forgives me for refusing the light hand,
and the soft lips, even as the sun fills the air with its first gold dust.

WAITING FOR HER TO WAKE

The first thing I see is the red cinnamon
flower bursting from the clay pot,
then the faint black bars of the railing,
the green sea, mountains beyond turning
into white limestone. And on the wine boat
now the dull whumps of full kegs rolling,
the sails down, voices of men
full of the quiet dawn they are passing.
But it is you, with your own morning,
and your brown hair weaving across the pillow,
and your child's lips, and your child's hands
before me. Suddenly
I see you are the world,
and I fear the moment
your eyes will open.

LINES OF RAIN

In this cold autumn I walk along the river
to watch the world of shadows cast by the trees
into the moving water. For hours our children
float by, incomplete seeds of our desire,
and for hours I remember holding you
in these wild flowers. Leafless, the willow bends
each branch to the wind, lines of rain
beat against the bark. Falling between me
and what I felt then, everything here
becomes insignificant except the beating
of my heart, green, and on fire.

THE ENCOURAGING SEA

After the fullness of the constellations settles in,
I go for a walk and remember the variations
of your name that day on the Atlantic Ocean,
how your tanned legs drifted like gold under water.
Then, nothing seemed to change; the lighthouse beam
circled, almost disturbing,
as we sat on the gray porch huddled over steaming cups of coffee.
Your eyes, your hands, the seagulls
that walked right up to our feet.

Yet the change began, the touching
but not touching that happened between us, and the sea,
shouting with its pink and blue-swirled shells,
and the long rifts of sand that said we had time.
So we sat, and ate, believing that was enough,
that we would come out more at night during the coming month
    to notice the moon,
that the words we floated toward each other
would remain as we said them.

CONSIDERING THE HOUSE

The house stands with its hundred years
in this rainy afternoon, seven windows broken
and boarded, double doors open,
behind it the green woods. You
believe we can tap mortar from the stone,
restore the slate roof, paint,
insulate, put kitchen cabinets
in the room facing south, open fireplaces,
the hardwood in back for burning.
The sky says no
and the clouds billowing within it say no
and I do not know what I am able to do
or not do, difficult
to even cross the patch of tall wet grass,
or peer into the guest house window.
It *is* magnificent: five bedrooms, six
large rooms downstairs, attic, cellar
with a spring, and you striding
the stairs despite bats, despite
the heavy cobwebs picked clean by the air,
despite the cherry tree limb that creaks, then cracks
and falls as we watch. Acres away
a farmer on a red tractor fades
smaller and smaller; hounds yelp
in fenced cages. I
can level the walls. Yes, I can run
the gray 100 amp wires. Yes, I can point
the stone, sand the floors
until they are smooth enough to walk on
with bare feet again. And you know I can.

WAKING AND REMEMBERING A FAMILY CEMETERY IN MAINE

The ocean sounds angry, but it is the bells of Orleans
that wake me to your face growing old so well,
like a chrysanthemum in November.
Without rising I watch the frontier of water shifting,
beyond which is a vast blue,
except for those few fishing boats
with men drawing nets up in silence.
For this moment it all makes sense,
the quiet of the long road in Maine, the coast,
the nine white stones sinking behind the white fence;
let me believe it will be like that, later, much later,
after many mornings like this, waking ourselves.

ON BIG JOHN'S HILL

Thousands and thousands of days
away, the poison sumac glows
in frozen clumps like dull, red balls
of blood, and I lift my knife
into the gray sky. Twisting, exotic,
the plum tree and the rusted pipes of the bridge
crossing the canal, and the huge, glistening
vines that have hung with green grapes all summer,
wait to see what I will do with my knife.
Unaware that I am once again the center,
I mindlessly carve my first initial,
a crooked white "L", into the living bark,
and then her initials, the "I" and "P"
much straighter, more exact;
and around them I struggle to make the perfect
heart.

WHITE PIGEON

for Gerald Stern

Every morning on the bare branch of December,
I pet the beak, stroke the lovely white neck.
There's a warm box for him in the hallway,
the blue blanket, water in the dead cat's dish.
I think of the feathers spread on pine needles,
the woodpecker big as my fist that woke me every morning,
the hundreds of blue and green parakeets twittering in the house-
    like cage in Italy
where the greasy rats ate from the feeder.

I crunch out into the snow in my pajamas,
in love with the delicate bending of his head,
the clumsy dancing circles on the branch.
I walk with my feet pointing out,
making bird tracks that darken and glitter;
my wife calls me back, yelling in whispers
so she won't wake the neighbors.
My children stand in the doorway pointing and laughing.
How can I go back, into the house,
for instant coffee, to shave, dress for work,
when in this world of white silence
I can reach into my shirt pocket, slowly, for him,
and scatter long arcs of the shining yellow seed?

THE DIVER AND THE COAL

My small piece of night, my
dry coal shining near fire,
my very shadow rising
from this dark earth.
Turning you this way
and that, I see you are the same
all over, as round as a marble, yet
faceted like a lover's words
in morning, a lover's face.
Someday I will forget about
work and eating hamburger, or
the clear, light thoughts
of October and November.
Someday I will dive into you,
and you will close,
and we will be gone.

CHILDREN SINGING

Startled by the few leaves
rattling on the birch, I look up,
see the stream's green edges frozen fast
with ferns and broken branches from the upland flood.
Darkness sifts the shagbark hickory, the black
walnut and blue spruces. Suddenly
the doves are still. Large,
white flakes flutter the air and I think
I may soon see them again,
the children, singing, their necks stretched
with a high, cathedral music in the breath-filled cold.
This time I won't ask them where they are going,
their faces blinking like candles in the trees;
this time I won't have to choose between the light in the evergreens
or stumbling after them, my body heavy with hope.
Snow will cover the gray barn's roof, the grainery's rusted dome,
and they will come, soft and light, clapping hands, dancing,
small souls who live wisely in the darkening cold.

WIND OVER LAND

For days notching and felling
trees, buzzing them into two-foot
pieces, hauling them to be split,
kneeling in leaves because here
I can hear the sea's murmur although
there is none. It is the wind over land
fallen like an angel that moves
the breath from my mouth like horses
in clouds, forming, rearing up and then
dissipating into the cold, clear air.
When I raise my eyes, everything is
in its place, looking back at me.

As soon as I began to know I sang,
the music turned outward, up into
the branches until they bristled
and snapped, and I stood absolutely
silent with the chain saw whirring
in my hands. This is my life, unheard
but singing and drifting out like those nights
I'd touch soft skin and beg to be touched
until I burned and still expected more. Still,
the silences are the same, my voice,
the burning, the sure movement of earth
waiting for what little I have to offer.

ANOTHER JOURNEY

Wind stirs small cedars,
snow lights on the ground.
There is a silence outside my window this morning
because soon you will not be able
to talk about busted knees or Polacks
or the browned woman you love
with sycamore or wing or sunlight;
you will not be able to say
you had nothing to do with it.

The quiet around your words
begs now to flow around your moon-white
bones, that will not open,
as you said they would. Not in daylight,
anyway, and not when somebody trying to prove something
is looking. I still hear you bend
the colt's breath to earth, the rain
onto snail shell and sparrow wingbone.

Now it's you
these black wings are gathering for,
and it's you they will bring finally
to that other shore,
Wheeling, West Virginia,
Bridgeport, Ohio.

III. FIRST ROOMS

RIDING OUT TO SEE THE FIRST FLOWERS

I watched you driving out into the green field
to see the flowers that first, warm March day,
your hand brushing away branches from the window,
the poison sumac bushes cracking, crows screaming,
flapping heavily up into trees,
until you hit the stump, muffler tearing off in blue smoke,
the car lurching downhill into the canal
where it coughed and sank.
Now dry mud crusts on sidewalks and stone walls,
dead birds lie caught
in this tail of the lion, this knot of calm and wind;
and you jut into the empy air,
float on the gray porch as you look
past the cobblestone path and stand of birches
to where they would bloom.
—They're gone the same way you're gone,
so quietly no one would have noticed
who hadn't walked out just after sunset
to watch the lake's breeze tilt the snow drops,
or hadn't seen the slanted lines of rain
bend or break their stems until
the petals splattered in the mud
where your dark hands lifted them, lightly,
and propped them up on forked twigs again.
Gone, like that day your baby-blue Buick's chrome
turned back the sun as you smoked up the hill,
tires beating down white rows of grass,
and I stood right where I'm standing now,
shading my eyes, wanting to follow.

PIP

The blacktop trucks, the French Canadians, my body sweating
as I raised the cold can of beer that morning I spent
with my grandfather, sitting on the truck's riding rails,
asking if he still made love to my grandmother,
and his laughing as he said, "At least once a week," snapped
    the thermos cap back on,
pulled the hydraulic jack, shifted those twenty tons of blacktop
    as though he were cradling a baby.
I remember feeling the power in his seventy-five-year-old fingers,
watching his eyes in the rear-view mirror as he jerked the truck's
    throttle and lowered the casing
to drive wherever we were working that day.
And I remember imagining the sadness of their bodies growing old
loving each other in that quiet bed on Olmstead Street,
under the white crucifix on the wall.

Some days I still see him picking up the rake,
putting his worn shoes into the hot stink until he's covered
    with oily fumes;
I see him stand straight and look at me, yell in his Canuck accent,
"Hey, young Roberts, you going to stand there all day?",
knocking me out of some emptiness I'd been staring at,
calling me, the fifteen-year-old he'd picked to be his wheelbarrow
    man,
and I'd add that extra thirty or forty pounds of blacktop,
even though working in sand or wet clay,
because I was bringing it to him.

38

WATCHING THE MOON

All morning I sit watching the cedar trees
in the barely moving July air,
and the red swingset poles, abandoned
in the field with coarse strings hanging
for the snowpeas which never come.
Tonight, about nine-thirty, I will see
the moon rising above the roof,
white as my mother's face, who I saw happy
for the first time just last month
when she came to visit, laughing,
posing for pictures like a young girl
who had not yet fallen in love.

Later it will be just the moon, old,
older than the deep love or scars
I've willed to another, or,
if not willed, given because of what I am;
and I will see that it's moved again,
as though its route were clear,
with me, or without.

DEAR MOTHER

I know this note is late but I'm sorry for your cold rooms
and seven sisters who never ate steak and potatoes,
I'm sorry for the winter you walked around in soft shoes.
If I sent this to you, would you put on your pink nightgown again
with the blue butterfiles on the sleeves,
move your arms up and down as you walk around the kitchen table
pretending you are an angel?

Here in Pennsylvania a lone yellow daisy stares at me awkwardly
over the lip of the rose-colored vase,
a gift from my love's daughter,
and the purple bird is poised motionless above it,
always about to sing, always about to flutter
its delicate, transparent wings.

Dear Mother
I am so exhausted I will have to sleep soon
and leave you alone again in the dark with your appendix scar
and fat white thighs and your stories about St. John's Alley.
The willow outside my window is not dripping in sorrow,
its branches are not bent, nor broken, but rather bowed
with the excessive waters of late winter and spring.

IT WILL WAIT

My brother lifts his tenth cup
of coffee into the haze
of WRGB favorite old time hits
and the maze of smoke from one
of his three packs of cigarettes,
says "Good morning" as though
he'd thought about it. "Good morning,"
I say back and look out the window
to snow that has piled to more
than three feet and it's time now
for the two of us to clear it. "Good
morning," he says again, and I repeat it,
then throw gloves, scarf and jacket
after him, see him as he leapt
from the airplane door, fingering the metal
clasps, the fine silken chute that would soon
Mae West in the blue,
bring him four, five times
faster home than he should go.
"Good morning," he says again and I say
"Shit." "No, it's a good morning,"
he repeats and I say, "Let's go, that snow's
not going to wait." But he sits
still, pours my coffee steaming
into the heavy white cup, adds the one spoon
of sugar, the quick spurt of cream,
says, "Here, have your cup of coffee.
The snow will wait."

THE UNBORN

If you come to me this late
day in March, I will bring you
to the room with six windows
full of north light in morning,
I will lift the black rose from the sidewalk
my mother swept every day, show you
the city of ants on rainbowed petals.
You've been alone so long now,
as long as I've been, but soon
you will cross the river of the unborn,
you will grasp the knot of confusion
tied in flesh, bring it out
from the sea you float in.
It is spring here and the world is alive
with shadows. Come out,
let me show you the raw, wet stones,
the fleshless moon, half shells
tossing in a dark sea.
Together we will bend
through the ivy and low branches,
whisper to the black crows walking dirt roads,
hear the sounds of snail,
and stone, the great wind
breathing.

JOSHUA

Cold, and the snow falls so steadily
the earth cannot bear any more,
and you are gone back after six weeks
to the dark. Delicate heads
of dried wheat stalks
bend with the light weight
and I see you curled in your mother's body
with praise never given.

Each flake tears a part of the dark sky into light;
I know a new loneliness tonight, and so
walk the white field, the darker woods,
which slowly fill with soundless snow.

THE DIFFERENCE

for Bradford

Tonight, in the middle of *Yertle the Turtle,*
just before the rocks speak,
you lay your damp head on the pillow and sink to sleep,
the green mobile stars above your bed
stirring in some breeze I can't feel.
I think someday we will be drinking,
or throwing a football in the yard
when suddenly you'll know again
that I am not your father,
that those nights spent holding warm on the couch,
or the times I scrambled eggs when your mother was gone,
even the afternoon I lifted you and your sister
to the pear tree's lowest branch, each of you on an arm,
were not moments of blood, just love.
And you will turn away, so slightly I may not notice,
and you will be gone—
but you may remember a man who slept
on your bed until morning, who bent
to kiss the eyelids that would soon flutter,
as though with breath, open.

THE INDIAN MAIDEN

Long rows of bare hickory trees
and a cold sun in February no one
would consider praising, clouds
moving apart the way you must be moving
by now into this hard ground.
This morning I thought about your weak heart,
the marble statue of the Indian Maiden
you climbed coming home from Boney's Bar,
singing her your favorite songs,
convinced that no woman could remain all stone.
Ten feet in the air you looked lonely,
loose-lipped, pigeons flapping around your head and shoulders,
cold hand raised against a beginning moon,
whispering in her ear.
I am alone here but almost dancing again
to your harmonica the way we danced
on the cracked linoleum, humming in the snow,
kicking dead leaves off your stone,
amazed at this gift of living and dying.

FIRST ROOMS

That night I stood watch over
the Polish ship docked in the harbor,
freezing in the dark with a pistol
cold against my skin, and rats big
as cats coming down the anchor ropes.
That night he came down to sell me bottles of vodka,
Polish hams, to give me dreams that last a lifetime.
43 cents a day
and if I jump ship they get my family.
His words, broken, darker than the shadows.

When I wake, it is Bethlehem, Pennsylvania
and my father has been walking
through Guadalcanal, through the Panama Zone.
He's been burying his brother again
so they won't tear his gold teeth out.
Holes are beginning in his skin
and the 105 degree fevers;
he is on fire in me, he is nothing
but a stone with entrance and withdrawal.

I lie here without sleeping.
That first night there was a seagull, dirty-white,
floating on the ocean waves. I thought
he must be freezing. But he rocked
and rocked, sometimes out of sight,
until I fell asleep leaning against a piling.

Buried in my nights, in my hands,
they are first rooms I keep coming back to.

IV. PARTISAN

PARTISAN

for Nikola Rudan

On the old road that is supposed to lead
to the sea, the gray sky
lights its way over the mountain.
Three kilometers down
the sea cove lightens,
sun inscribes scrub pines,
moves like a tongue into the white house.

Last night a man there told me about his brother,
a doctor drafted from this island
to treat typhus-ridden Partisans on the coast,
showed his picture, the strong-boned face,
the lid drooping on a glass eye—
the only way later the mother could identify the son,
and so carry the scratched burnt orb back to bury near roses;
told me how they would sail at night with explosives tied
to rowboats, wineboats, fishing craft already half-sunk,
how they would jump into the Adriatic
and pray the rope on the tiller would hold,
wait for the explosion.

Two men of every three from this island
had their names engraved on the plaque under the fig tree;
and the mayor of Bogomolje nods into the air,
the Partisan's brother shouts Tito, Roosevelt, Krsto, Pavitsa,
    Pavao,
the delicate dead in names about to burst.

STONE BUILDER ON HVAR

In this place of stone I work with stone,
cut the square large blocks,
drag them with donkeys here where I can chip
and place them in the walls of my growing house.
As for the wineboat men who carry our casks
to the mainland's hotels, or the teenaged girls
who change into suits at the tip of the cove,
I watch them and welcome them but am glad
when they're gone. For it is the veins of stone
and jagged edges, the quick
crystals and weight that tell me I have a soul.
I have thought about this often,
the hum of bees circling the island,
the six goats and moon big as the cistern,
all lead only to when my hands,
thick with mortar, lift
to place another stone.

VIDE UNFOLDING NETS

As soon as the sea turns calm
I unfold the nets,
throw minnow cans into the boat
and row out into the sun. The gulls scream,
like Magda or Radka, and even the goats,
when the moon comes full, scream, until
the limestone cliffs ring and seem to rise.
I saw the Germans climb those cliffs. Squatting,
I watched my father bead on one and fire,
and gravity pull four, five times harder
at his body until he blew backward into the sea.
Here nothing moves and the light turns purple, rich
blue, green, sometimes gray, sometimes gull white. I
could row and row these nights, the green light
on my bow dipping, no mosquitoes out so far,
and think about the Greeks and Yugoslavs
while I drink my wine. Some day
I will not be able to pull my boat in
and I will drift all the way down,
past even the town where, when I was eighteen,
I had a woman and drank all week,
and came home to smile and tell no one.

OLD WOMAN ON HVAR

Nothing but sea and eels on Saturday nights
and limestone cliffs that dry my skin
even more than my eighty-six years, and still
I enjoy sitting here on the milking stool
while the tourists gape and my great-
granddaughter washes and combs the thick lines
of my white hair. Nothing changes
and everything changes, and my son
is old now and his son the age of Pavao
when we danced on this same veranda
more than seventy years ago. Oh, the red
cinnamon flower and long swim
to the Virgin waiting at the end
of the cove to welcome home the tired men
and to welcome us as we climbed the cutting rocks
to the scrub pine clearing and lay down.
The sea talked, and we listened,
even when the Italians came and made him crawl
through the town's center,
even when they tore my clothes off
and forced themselves into me.
—I'm telling you we walked the island's sixty-three kilometers
one summer, camping in the dusty fields of lavender,
telling everyone we were doing it for fun. Children
ran to us from the stone huts, strangers
gave us fish, tomatoes.
And at night the stars, always the stars,
jagged, sharp, trembling like ships
in the heat's haze as they sailed down the channel.
—When he died I put on the black skirt and blouse,
the black bandana and shoes. I looked like a crow
walking from village to village for odd jobs
and firewood, waiting for my son to grow.
And there he is now, my son, just
coming in from catching eels,
his hand up for a good three or four
seconds, waving.

ONE DREAM OF TWO RED STARFISH

Slowly the sea took over
and made us move in sleep
the way we'd walk after swimming
for hours or fishing in the anchored boat.
But we have no boat here, and no water,
only the dark rhythm of our breathing
dreams against each other, one starting
up from the damp sheets, one
turning back into the pillow. I
will never ask what your dream was,
but listen: two red starfish,
one twice as large as the other,
sucked on the green rock
as water drifted over; they felt
pushed and pulled by the changing
cloud shapes of fish and sun. That
was years ago. When I came back
the smaller one was there alone,
still clinging, brilliant orange-red.
I rowed in that cove for days,
leaning over, black sea-mask on,
until my spine ached. I was out there
when fine rain pitted the water with craters,
clouds piled blue-gray and wind
blew cold on my skin. I stayed
a full night thinking the flashlight
would pick up the gleam, the trace.
Listen: I never found him. Listen:
I'm afraid because the dream brought such pain,
but I will never ask what your dream was.

ENJOYING THE ENGLISH COUNTRYSIDE

Tall, green grass and slow boats
move as though in grass, and the thick
brown body of the canal
curves into sight and then is gone.
One man stands straight up into the heavy
clouds and waves as the sun sends
one tunnel of light down.
I have never seen so many steeples
and statues, and you
love the quiet red flowers. I love
your purple and blue embroidered skirt,
the fine, thin hair pulled back and up
from your high-boned face. Even
in England my French and Indian
and Irish bloods race
and I want to lay you down onto the thick grass
where your white legs might close
like wings around me.

HERCULES' TEMPLE AT PAESTUM

Standing in one shaft
of shadow, the old man explains
they cannot build a road
because every time they begin to dig,
more ruins are exposed. To build
a road here would be a shame anyway,
waking the long bones of the dead
to these exhaust fumes billowing
where lions ate them
and the sun is eating us.
Raising his tiny, gnarled hands,
shaking his head with short, quick
"no's," he leaves snorting, as though
we were to blame. But after the wine
at the Paestum Hotel, after cursing the mosquitoes
and the Romans for being dumb enough
to build their town on a marsh—
not believing the river could ever
change its course—
we still come back to stand under these columns
of Hercules' Temple. And in the last red glow
the snail shell in your hand is a ruin,
and we are ruins
surrounded by air-stepping brown and green lizards,
grains wind-whittled from the pillars,
and the stillness of those who came here before us.

THE RAPE OF THE SABINE WOMEN

We find them in the Great Square,
the dark churches, on the walls decayed
with years. The woman
flying up, her long white arm
flowing from her body, the body
of her lover or husband
low to the pedestal of ground, the other
man lifting her, a weightless,
wingless human bird in his hands.
Who are they and where
did they come from, and where
was he taking her, you ask
as we sit at the cool table.
But I can only say my brother
was raped in leaves by a dying river,
my mother raped white as these statues
by the hard stones and hard lives
of St. John's Alley, that my father
raped himself until he could not come home
without the bottles. That everyone of us
rapes the other until not even the victorious
David, not even the long, cold face of Dante,
can watch any longer the frantic soaring
her once human body makes,
how greatly she strives to fly away
from this earth.

WALKING THROUGH A FAMILY GRAVEYARD AND THINKING OF THE ITALIAN STONE BUILDERS

Well, I'm not dead, not yet,
although parts of me have died
and stayed dead.
The black spider, who is her own night,
stretches her legs as wide as my palm
and builds her web among these dead. She
ignores me and the gray sky and,
by the way her legs are thrumming,
I imagine her singing the way the Italian
stone builders must have been singing
when they built Vaux-le-Vicomte for Fouquet
and, later, Versailles for the King. They
couldn't care who the owner was, only care
for the orange and blue and white veins running
their courses through the gray rock,
and the weight of the stone block
as they lifted it, and set it,
gently, into place.

BEHIND THE COUNTER AT A SODA SHOP IN FLORENCE

He has always been here, as far
as I can see. All the time
examining the carved silver and gold
on the Ponte Vecchio, and
all those hot minutes of sun spent
deciding whether to go back to our dark
room and love or to go see
some other statue,
he was right here, with the shimmering
mirrors and polished brass
handles. Thousands-of-years-
chiseled nose and chin, tanned
skin over rounded arms and shoulders, long
muscles down the lovely neck and back and buttocks
to the curved legs, he
is what they made from all those nights
awake thinking of the white
moon and black sea, more
lovely than marble.
I knew him, and I watched you
knowing him, and I watched him
minding his own business, dipping
the ice-cream smeared glasses into the sink,
scrubbing the cups, the knives and spoons,
the delicately etched glass plates.

CATCHING EELS

For Krsto Rudan

Half-tumbling down the cracked concrete steps
to where the old fishing boat lurches
against its rope, Vide throws first the wound net,
then the pail of glittering sardines, and last,
with the gentlest motion, the skin flask
of red wine that he will raise
and drink in the moon's shadow. Out there,
on the channel sea that barely
ripples, he hears his dead brother, the first
whimper, the second, the third, until he is lost
in the counting and so stops
and listens and stares.
He remembers his brother,
how he slept with the sick, gave them his water,
wrote letters for them, wrote himself
to women that their husbands, or sons,
fathers or lovers were dead . . .
how the soldiers dug him a separate grave,
would not throw his body into the general ditch.
—And when Vide lights his good American cigarette,
he sees the night is going and it is time
to snap the firm flesh of sardine onto the three-
pronged hooks, one-hundred-and-twenty flapping bodies
beating the bottom of his leaking boat,
one-hundred-and-twenty silver lights lifted,
thrown into the lightening channel
where the big fish swim. And he sits, rocking,
listening for the music that is under
all water; he waits for it to begin.